Time Again

Time Again

An Essay on Zhuangzi, Fatherhood,
and Other Matters of Life and Death
as They Concerned the Author
on a Visit to Northeastern Oregon

Scott F. Parker

SHANTI ARTS PUBLISHING
BRUNSWICK, MAINE

Time Again
An Essay on Zhuangzi, Fatherhood, and Other Matters
of Life and Death as They Concerned the Author
on a Visit to Northeastern Oregon

Copyright © 2023 Scott F. Parker

All Rights Reserved
No part of this document may be reproduced or
transmitted in any form or by any means without prior
written permission of the publisher, except in the case
of brief quotations embodied in critical reviews.

Published by Shanti Arts Publishing

Cover and interior images by Scott F. Parker
and used with his permission

Shanti Arts LLC
193 Hillside Road
Brunswick, Maine 04011
shantiarts.com

Printed in the United States of America

ISBN: 978-1-951651-72-3

Library of Congress Control Number: 2022952451

for August, for always

"That which gives life to life does not live."
—Zhuangzi

Strange dream last night. I woke up just as the Dalai Lama was saying that he had tried but failed to live his life in the shallows. I had a hunch what he meant: despite a lifetime of meditation, thoughts still interfered with his ability to meet the world as it is.

But it was my dream, wasn't it? One way or another, this was a story I was telling myself.

There is just enough early morning light for me to see my way to the water. My gear lies beside my tent ready to go. I pull on my shorts and haul my board down to the lakeshore. There's no one else around. Water so still it might be solid, yet as I push off from the beach, it gently adjusts its contours to accommodate mine. Working together, we propel the board forward, letting it glide easily toward the middle of the lake. Pretty soon I'm out over deep water.

And before I know it, I'm submerged. The water is cold. Not as cold as I would have imagined, but cold. Rising to the surface, I take a deep reassuring breath and pull myself up onto my board.

I don't know what caused me to fall. I reflect on the moments prior. The water had been calm. I had been standing on my board until—suddenly—I was wet. Beyond this I come up blank. Whatever caused the fall is a mystery to me. I appear to have been pushed around by forces, whether physical or mental (Did my wandering attention cause me to fall?), beyond my ken.

Water drips steadily from my clothes as the wind picks up, an hour till sunrise.

I was only a few hours out of Bozeman when Sandy called. The doctors were now telling her that the baby wasn't growing as much as he was supposed to and likely would not make it to full term. It hurt to hear the worry in her voice and to feel it in my heart.

Was there a beginning to my unborn son? A beginning to that beginning? How did, how does, how can being begin?

I sit on a fallen log at Lolo Pass wondering if the deer I scared from the trail a few minutes ago will pass this way again.

Alone for now, answering only to myself, time stretches out like the expanding universe. There is time to wait for a deer that might not come; time, when a log presents itself, to take a seat; time to let my environment shape my day. And the more time there is, the slower it moves.

The closer I come to the asymptote on the horizon, the more I fade away.

The self lives in time and time only. Examine a moment: no one is there. But take any two moments, and there is the self staring back in need. Zero equals zero; yet zero plus zero equals one. If the self doesn't exist in *zero*, it must be in the *plus*.

Peace, like pain, is one of those experiences of which abstraction gives not even a taste.

Time passes from now to now, and still it is now.

I must first be lost to be found, but once I am found, I was never truly lost. If life made more sense to me, I fear I'd be making too much of it. The point isn't to make sense but to make my way down the trail.

Among these immense trees, some of the western redcedars are three thousand years old, growing slowly, reacting but never overreacting to their environments. When there's a break in the canopy, grow toward the light. When it's your time to be replaced, let yourself be the stuff from which what replaces you will draw nutrients. As you decay, your descendants will root themselves in your remains. The past is *in* the present, the present is *planted* in the past. What trees, what trees!

One tree in this forest is called Scott. It comes up from the earth like every other tree. It goes back to the earth like every other tree.

My experience is like the late afternoon sunlight glistening on the shallow wide river, my experience is the late afternoon sunlight glistening on the shallow wide river.

Driving west, I'm listening to Dylan as the heat ticks higher. All around me are the telltale signs that in the doorway of life stands death.

Time not out of mind: When Lewis and Clark came this way and the Nez Perce wondered if the hair on their pale faces revealed their descent from dogs and nevertheless greeted them with magnanimity.

Here in the northeastern corner of Oregon, I loose myself among mountains, forests, and canyons. In my satchel are Burton Watson's *Complete Works of Zhuangzi* and the notebook I'm writing in now. Nothing more would fit. What more would I want?

There are enough butterflies here that I think Zhuangzi must be teasing me.

Am I dreaming when I imagine that if I weren't thinking of butterflies there wouldn't be any? And if I weren't thinking of Zhuangzi? And if I weren't thinking of myself? A thought is made by people thinking it; things are so because they are called so.

Partway down Hells Canyon, I'm seated on the bended trunk of a tree growing out of the Imnaha River. My feet are in the water, which is as cool as the air is warm. The swallowtails are impressive in size as well as number. They give a certain primordial feel that suits the remoteness of this place and the vastness of this deep canyon.

The campground here is named for the warrior Oolokot, younger brother of Young Joseph, chief of the Wallowa band of Nez Perce, both sons of Tuekakas (Old Joseph). From the perspective of the old-growth ponderosas now giving me shade, these men were just here.

But I am not a tree; how do I know the tree's perspective? I know it by standing here beside it.

Thoughts grow in the mind like leaves on a tree. Last year's leaves are dead; there's no reason to hang onto them. So forget the years.

A tree is not a "tree"; a tree is a tree. This, I think, is the meaning of not thinking. But what I think is only what I think, not what I don't think, which I already forgot.

My feet dip in and out of the river. I am not searching for equilibrium; I am enjoying cold and hot, the one then the other, each moment a contrast with the one that preceded it. Like thirst before drink, absence sharpens the senses. Going without makes it possible to accept what's given. The apple I'm eating is as good as any apple I've tasted. Better. Such is the present.

An ongoing global pandemic, politics on the brink of national immolation, the forests literally immolating around us—what kind of world is this? What kind of life for a child?

We might have debated having another child indefinitely, but sometimes nature has its way, and the rest of the time never happened.

A gust of wind. The ponderosas drop their orange buds into the water, where they bob along as the water dictates. Aren't we all orange buds bobbing down the river? I have never known any life but the one that keeps unfolding with me. What will come for the little orange buds? We will see—or we won't. The mystery is theirs as much as it is ours.

And so we rush headlong into the future. The baby is coming, and the world will be as it is, as has always been so. It is possible our new son's life will be worse than Sandy's and mine. It is also possible that it will be better. But better and worse are not the standards of life. The standard of life is life itself.

"Come in," says the mystery. "Welcome."

You don't have to say yes. But you don't have to say no either.

The impression the river gives is of flowing from a source that will never be depleted or of something coming perpetually from nothing, notices the man sitting in the tree, and saying to the water, "We're not so different, you and I."

If I had a watch, it would measure an hour to be the same in the woods as it is in the city. But the hour here makes no demands. I move from the tree by the river when my butt gets sore. I sit on a mat under a different tree. I listen to the river and the birds and the flies when they come by. It doesn't bother me that I don't know what I'm doing here. With nowhere to go, all I can do is stay and see what happens.

Back to the river, where I am standing knee-deep in the water under the shade of the trees. If I knew the source of the river, what would I know? Given enough time, the questioning mind can find everything but satisfaction.

Before the river was a river, it was not a river; there was no river. Before the river was a river, it wasn't even not a river.

I want to meet my son, whoever he is. I am his father, whoever he will be. His nature, whatever it is, flows right through me.

Sandy and I ensured him death in the same moment we gave him life. Listen to me: "gave him life"—like he was just sitting around waiting for it.

But, yes, he will die. What is done is undone. Only the timeless does not die, and our son like all sons will be born in time. We in our love hoisted time upon the timeless. Life, then, is love. And if life is love, then death, too, is love. And the opposite of love? Nothing.

Maybe Buddha gave up his family for eternity. Maybe Christ demanded it of his followers. Maybe for them family was not worth the price of life and death and time. Maybe if God himself came to me in the recesses of this canyon and offered me a ticket to heaven, I'd give the ticket back.

In the clear solitude of the canyon, I choose my wife, my born son, and my unborn son. If the canyon teaches me that I am always alone, it is only existentially so.

Part of the pleasure of being alone in the wilderness is the pleasure of anticipating having been alone in the wilderness.

The temptation of time, the temptation not to be present, is a strong temptation.

Even to distinguish time and timelessness is to do what can only be done *in time*. Prelapsarian, undifferentiated reality cannot be regained. Recognized, perhaps, but not regained. The fruit of the tree of time cannot be uneaten. The trick, therefore—as if logic had a thing to do with it—is to be both timeless and in time, to be *fully* alive and *fully* that which isn't born and doesn't die. How to pull off that trick beats me.

Ideas are just ideas. The sun is behind the canyon ridge now, and rainclouds are moving in quickly. It might be a storm. It might not be a storm.

Zhuangzi teaches me nothing; better, he makes me laugh!

What is the river saying? you ask.

I knew exactly what the river was saying.
Right up to the moment you asked, I knew.

I keep looking at this particular ponderosa next to my tent. Its bark is almost pink in the light. This tree, never trying to be anything but what it is and not even trying to be that, just being it. I say my thanks, but the tree is too busy to answer. This tree—a million like it and none the same.

A tree is not a "tree"; a tree is a tree. A "tree" is a thought, I think, a thought I think.

What is the meaning of life? What is the meaning of a tree? A tree is a tree! And so a life is a life. When we speak of meaning we pull away from what is. But this is no plea on behalf of silence; this is a plea on behalf of being over meaning, a plea for language as well as for silence, language that adopts the grammar of the butterfly's path, language that breaks the cage of literalism, language that is as language does, humans being as humans do.

The world must be made in contrast. Mountains, canyon. Land, water. Presence, absence. Being, nonbeing. Form, emptiness. If not the world, beauty. Conflict, harmony.

I turn around where the road ends, at the Hells Canyon Dam. Both lanes were clear just a few minutes ago. But now, as I drive south, a rockslide blocks the northbound lane. Lucky to be where I am when I am, I barely slow down.

An unapologetic turkey vulture on the shoulder of the road, a rafter of turkeys on the move, an osprey in wait, deer and rabbits here and there, two racer snakes racing from the trail, evidence of bears in two fresh piles of digested berries on the ground here in berry paradise.

There's mid-eighties and then there's mid-eighties. This morning's hike on the Kinney Creek Trail was cooked with menace, but it's cool now as a noontime rain passes through the canyon.

Back on the Oregon side of the river, at Copperfield Park, I inflate my board in a light rain, which vanishes to the east as I take the water.

Below the Oxbow Dam that has helped decimate the anadromous fish of time immemorial, the river still moves. Careful or I fall. Not too careful or I don't get off the shore. It is balance I need, the balance of breathing from my heels.

I sense that if I were to breathe like Zhuangzi's True Man my mind might descend from my head to my body to the water supporting me. And then, perhaps, even if I were to fall I wouldn't get wet.

I don't notice any fish until I learn how to see them. Then there they are, right below me. Big fish—trout, catfish—that, if I'm honest, scare me a little. What would they teach me if I could go with them? How deep is the mystery in which they swim?

The relief of not having access to the internet is not easily overstated.

Now go further: imagine if there were nothing tugging you away from where you are. How long could you stay?

Solitude, like stillness, is a test. There is no passing the test or failing. But there is taking the test and examining the results.

If consciousness exists, it has always existed. I can't prove it. My mind goes blank there. But it seems right to me.

By analogy: Life has always existed. If it came out of the elements, it was in the elements. And if the elements came out of the Big Bang, the elements were in the Big Bang.

Something from nothing began before the beginning, and our accounts, our explanations, our words will not change this.

Nobody telling the trees where to grow, the water where to flow, the ants where to go. And in having no "right" way to do things, they never do anything the wrong way. We are this way, too, if we notice: always already free.

No schedule, no responsibilities, no commitments. When, then, to stop? When, then, to begin? When, then, to change?

Without hesitation, without delay, without a moment's thought, without question.

Life happens but not to us. It happens through us as we happen through it.

One happening after another happening. A happening doesn't happen until it happens. Then it's happening. All around, it's happening right now.

In the future I will look back on this trip with fond feelings, but right now I'm feeling fondly for any number of gone-away times. Solitude is a test, and silence can sometimes be like thunder.

My awareness goes away from me, revealing that I am a phenomenon of some kind, a phenomenon that I don't have to identify with. It doesn't last long, this revelation. I try to hold on to my understanding, which only squeezes the life right out of it.

I wake up in my tent and reach immediately for a book. Habit is habit and ideas are ideas. But ideas are just ideas. I put the book down and listen to Lick Creek, having no idea what its sound means. None. Nor these early-morning birds. Nor Zhuangzi and his beautiful nonsense. Nor even the sound of my own name. Never mind it all. What more would we ask of the creek?

The pleasures of town are always clearer upon
returning to them: the bushes in the planters,
the stones in the patio, the bricks in the wall,
the shade under a tree, the coffee in my cup.

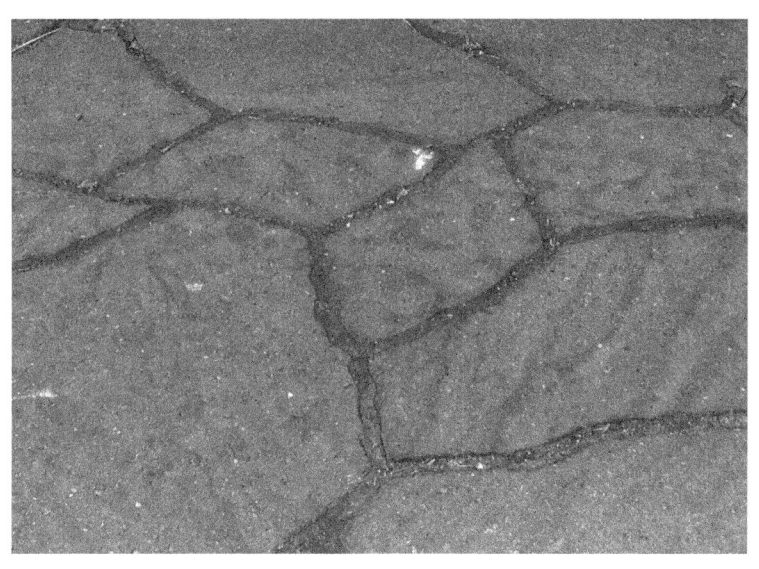

Life isn't fair. Life is life.

Haven't you noticed that life is purposeless? Absurd, really. If it were news it would be good news.

Don't you remember you were present when the universe was born? Ridiculous! Madness! Unthinkable! Delightful!

Sitting by Wallowa Lake reading a biography of Chief Joseph, I look around in recognition. Home isn't what you know; home is what knows you.

Why would I want to feel like I'm on the water when I can be *on the water?*

It's possible to try too hard, Zhuangzi tells me. Follow your bliss, says Joseph Campbell, it may lead you to your nature. When you need a week alone in the wilderness, take it. When it's time to paddle, paddle.

I go out at sunset as the boats are coming in and paddle out where no one is and bob along the surface of the lake, feeling the water's movement beneath my feet, trying to keep balance as the waves come by, knowing finally that it isn't up to me. The eagle cry comes from far off. I can just make out a white dot in the trees and paddle toward it. The eagle takes no notice of me, perched as it is above the lake keeping watch. I sit on my board and watch until it is too dark to see, then I listen to the eagle cry in the dark night. Years ago, it might have been my father on the water listening. Years from now, it might be my sons.

When we choose life and death, do we not choose the dream over reality, asked the disciple.

The master smiled and asked in reply if the distinction between the dream and reality were not itself another dream.

So, what is real, the disciple asked. Anything? What is real and what is really real?

What is real, said the mater, is what we call real. And what is really real is what we don't call real.

Unseen, in their midst was the witness, who did not say, What a shame. The disciple is so earnest, the master is so satisfied, and they both forget that the original question had to do with life, death, and eternity. Is the temporal a dream? Is the eternal real? But the real dream is that there is a choice to be made or anyone to make it.

In the morning I return to the eagle's tree, say good morning, and paddle on.

An hour later, sunrise approaching, I return again to the tree and watch as the eagle delicately lifts its tail feathers and squirts a shit on the bushes below. And then I hear the whooshing of its wings as it hops to the next branch on the tree and begins the elaborate ritual of refolding its wings. A lot of trouble, it seems, for such small returns.

Walking around Iwetemlaykin, I come to the cemetery where Tuekakas has lain since he was moved from Wallowa, where his sons buried him, after that grave was twice robbed. Before he died, he told Joseph, "This country holds your father's body. Never sell the bones of your father and your mother."

Out on the water at noon, what but one of those big Oregon swallowtails I've been seeing flies out over the water and keeps my pace just a few feet to my side. What for these moments is the relationship between us? Could it be that we are dreaming the same dream? And where does the butterfly go? Alone again, I paddle to deep water and sit down on my board to look at the shore and feel the sun on my back.

One by one, the doctors have retracted their various diagnoses, and we are back to thinking of the baby the only way we ever wanted to: as healthy, as normal. But if he had trisomy, he would have trisomy; if he were a dwarf, he'd be a dwarf; and if he were a potato, he'd be a potato. If his left arm were a rooster, he could keep watch on the night. From what void inside ourselves do we summon words like "normal"?

My tent is pitched in a forest full of smoke. I breathe in the only air available to me. And I think the thoughts that surface, the only thoughts available to me.

Solitude doesn't just reveal my nature; it expresses it, too. I need to be alone periodically because I'm someone who needs to be alone periodically. Nature is always emerging from nature. My unborn son, his nature, too, is emerging.

By definition, solitude cannot be shared. Whatever it gives me, it gives only to me. And to share its gifts is to transform them, to represent publicly what can only be private. But such, of course, is the way of all experience.

The words you read don't mean the same thing as the words I write. Nevertheless, what kind of experience do I hope you will have in these pages?

Dear unborn son, I hope it is not too much to wish that these words might draw you into an appreciation of your own, that my reflections present to you an occasion for your own, that you might receive my love for you and extend it when you're ready to someone you have not yet met, that you might see in my exploration of nature an angle of approach to your own.

I will go now and sit on the bank of the Madison and watch the river flow as the sun sets. And if I know myself at all, as I sit I will think of other rivers I have had the fortune to sit by and of other people who have had the fortune to sit by this one. One way or another, son, I will be thinking of you.

The ouroboros never starts eating its tail and never stops. It only and always is eating its own tail. I'd say that's the idea, but that would be another idea, which would have nothing to do with it. I'd say that's the idea, but it isn't.

Concepts of reality are fine if you are interested in concepts but are not much help if you are interested in reality.

Let the scientists know about things. Let the philosophers know about knowing. Let us be.

Down by the river the sun has set and the insects are out on the water. Trout rise to catch them. The songbirds are taking an encore. The wind has changed and to the southeast the sky is almost blue. I take one last look at the water before returning to camp. And what do I see in my one last look? The nature of time itself already a memory. The mystic may be right that there is that which does not arise and pass away, but we will never know it.

Every day a man goes to the woods to be at one with nature. And every day when he gets there he spends all this time thinking, wondering why he isn't one with nature, asking himself what it will take, determined to find the answer.

Forget what you've learned. It'll be like you never knew.

Just as our flight is approaching Los Angeles, the plane plunges toward the ground before shooting violently back skyward. As this continues, we clip trees, then surge vertical before completing a backflip. Down and up we go. The pilot, who turns out to be the Dalai Lama, comes over the loudspeaker and in a perfectly calm voice explains that there is a problem, that the crew is working on it, and that if they can't fix it we'll go down in fifteen minutes. There's plenty of booze onboard, he adds, for anyone who wants it. Then, calm as ever, he begins confessing to his dead mother. I pity my fellow travelers who will choose to avail themselves of the booze instead of listening. What, I wonder, could be better preparation for death? The Dalai Lama's voice is tender toward his mother; the exchange is intimate; the wisdom sure to be profound: I have tried and failed, he tells her, to live my life in the shallows.

I woke up before the plane went down. The voice was calm as water, but the dream was over. I woke up and went down to the lake.

If it wasn't my dream, whose was it?

Scott F. Parker is the author of several books, including *Being on the Oregon Coast* and *A Way Home: Oregon Essays*, as well as the editor of *Conversations with Ken Kesey* and *Conversations with Joan Didion*. He teaches writing at Montana State University and is the nonfiction editor for Kelson Books.

photo: Alyssa Henry

www.ingramcontent.com/pod-product-compliance
Lightning Source LLC
Chambersburg PA
CBHW042131160426
43198CB00022B/2976